Inland Sea

Inland Sea

Poems by

Lynn Domina

Cover design by Shay Culligan
Cover image by Nemuel Sereti
Author photo by Sandra K. Jones

ISBN: 978-1-63980-366-8

Kelsay Books
502 South 1040 East, A-119
American Fork, Utah 84003
Kelsaybooks.com

For my mother and in memory of my father,
Elizabeth and Dean Domina

Acknowledgments

The author wishes to thank the editors of the following magazines, anthologies, and other publications in which these poems first appeared, occasionally in slightly different form.

Alaska Quarterly Review: "Inside"
Barrow Street: "The Dreamer's Wish Is Never Fulfilled in the Dream"
The California Quarterly: "Mixed Media: Grief"
Christian Century: "One Dragonfly Hovers"
Dunes Review: "Three Views of Flight"
Educe: "Seven Meditations on Romance"
Fjords Review: "Archipelago"
Free State Review: "Year of Water"
Gettysburg Review: "No Dinosaur Ever Saw Superior," "Blue Hope"
Green Mountains Review: "The Decent Thing"
Hiram Poetry Review: "Illustrated Cookbook"
Hyphenate: "The Poet Responds to Her Lover, the Painter Who Claims Words Languish Beside Color, Texture, Shadow and Light"
Kenyon Review: "Do Carnivorous Plants Experience Hunger?"
Marquette Monthly: "Bear"
Massachusetts Review: "That Delicious Word"
The Museum of Americana: "After Reading John S. Willett's *Book of American Trivia*"
New England Review: "I've Heard Stories"
New Letters: "Literacy"
Nimrod: "Water Music, 7-17-1717," "Bear"
Pembroke: "Golden Gate"
Portland Review: "Northern Michigan, Late Afternoon, Early September"
Presence: "McCarty's Cove"
Quartet Journal: "After Learning to Tie a Boat with a Rolling Hitch"

River Heron Review: "Chant to Lift Up the Soul of George Floyd"
River Styx: "Blood"
Salamander: "Foreground"
Tiferet: "Every River Remembers the Drowned"
Valparaiso Poetry Review: "Wreath," "Boundary Water"
Vita Poetica Journal: "White Deer"
Whale Road Review: "Mockingbird"
Zone 3: "Wetlands," "Peregrination"

Connoisseurs of Suffering: Poetry for the Journey to Meaning:
    "Golden Gate"
The Donut Anthology: "First Breakfast in Weihai"
Maiden Voyage: "Bear," "The Road to Happiness"
The Practicing Poet: "Eye to Eye," "Three Views of Flight"
Rewilding: Poems for the Environment: "Do Carnivorous Plants
    Experience Hunger?"
Superior Voyage: "Chant to Lift up the Soul of George Floyd,"
    "McCarty's Cove," "No Dinosaur Ever Saw Superior"
    "Wetlands," "White Deer"
Waters Deep: A Great Lakes Poetry Anthology: "Inland Sea,"
    "Burned"

"Moose" and "The Road to Happiness" were originally published as broadsides by Winter Cabin Press.

Contents

I

Shoreline

i.
My favorite days, I cannot identify
blue that is water, blue that is sky,
blue that is horizon.

ii.
I crave this lake's chill,
pain thrilling my legs,
back, wrists, those minutes
I remain fully immersed.

iii.
You can see one small cave,
hollowed by erosion, only
if you've left the path,
understanding that if you step
even farther, you'll stumble or the overhang
will collapse. Either way,
you'll likely die.

iv.
Three chunks of driftwood
have landed together
where sand meets stone,
broken shells beside them
reflecting green sea glass.

v.
I've been wanting to create
more words
to name *blue*.

vi.

My best stones
turn out to be slag, pocked
by air bubbles that burst
when bits of ore
tumbled into frigid water.

vii.

Late spring, discs of ice
swirl within a half-moon cove.

viii.

Some truth resides
in storm-driven waves
but I can't discern completely
what it is.

ix.

Winter afternoons we climb
ice banks so far out
we forget which world
is safe, which dangerous.

Passage

Some of my ancestors stayed
in France and some in Canada
and some stayed in Maine, along the coast.
In Canada, they stayed
in Quebec, adapted
their accents if not their language.

My ancestors' children moved
to Quebec City and Montreal I imagine.
A great uncle resents his girth wedged
against streetcar seats, resents
the seats and the woman behind him
humming to her infant. He married
wealth, can't forget
what isn't his. Fifty years back an aunt,
maybe an in-law, locks her child
in a cellar, leaves
him there until her hands stop shaking.
A cousin many times removed
hosts dinner parties for friends who call him
the American because he lacks imagination
cursing. That's me, the American,

living as far north now as I can get
without becoming Canadian, putting down roots
inland, beside another sea. I don't speak
a word of French, can't ask
directions to the Museum of Natural History,
order a slate of bread and cheese,
or even curse whatever it is
that leaves me so vexed
with the filter I've installed
to screen the past.

After Learning to Tie a Boat with a Rolling Hitch

That was the day we argued—
or debated, or discussed—which was better. *The Iliad*
you said, battle after battle after battle,
one big bloody mess I said, but you liked Achilles
and his love for, who was it, Hector,
no, Patroclus. *The Odyssey,* I said, clever
Odysseus calling himself
Nobody, remembered all these millennia,
as if any warrior would claim he's nobody,
as strained by society's getting and spending
as Emily Dickinson who wasn't nobody
either but had a mind
to be. Odysseus strapping his men
to the warm gurgling bellies
of sheep, blinding the Cyclops, a creature
my high school friend confused,
by way of ogre, I kid you not, with orgy.
And who doesn't envy Circe, turning
those men into pigs, revealing
in their physical form their inner natures,
and so you asked me
what Circe could turn me into, what outward form my
inner nature would take. I thought for a minute
until I saw it, Aeolus' bag of wind, wind
tactile if not exactly visible—don't
scold me for deflecting your question—oh, western wind
soft as spring clover, a gust, a breeze, or wild
as the wine-dark sea.

Moose

I noticed the word
on a map, the word
peculiar as the spindly-legged
animals it names. I saw the word
laid across green flats
west of Marquette,
its pitch sonorous as grief, its meaning
indistinct—one or two or many.
I imagined the word
lying down like a moose, her legs
hinged beneath her,
nestled in silvery grass. I imagined
its timbre rising up
as a moose, letters
gathered into antlers, into bulky jaw and haunch,
rounded into nostrils snorting mist,
fringed into coarse fur. I admit
my hope—to see
an actual moose lumbering
through birch and maple and pine
as my map assured me—
she or they remain,
brown shoulders sliding into deep shadow,
faint as an idea
but warm with muscle and pelt
and breath.

Field Work

I began with trees, listening
to rattles and whispers,
breezes rustling their leaves.
I fingered their bark, distinguishing
oak from maple, aspen from birch,
beheld fir, juniper, cedar.
Some evergreen needles
swooped down softly, rested
pliably in my own hand.

I noticed nests and eggs and birds,
recognized robins of course. A blue
half-shell had landed
among our hostas, urging
life into the future. I delighted
at the pileated woodpecker who lived two days
behind our garden, oak shavings
floating into our compost. I already knew
jays would bully chickadees,
and I already knew grackles
were smaller than crows and more
iridescent, but what about that brown one,
its tail specked white, and what about
that other brown one, its wings striped white?
I listened as my friends described
silhouettes of red-tailed hawks or turkey buzzards
in flight. All I'd known was that the word
buzzard repulsed me. Featherless heads
evolved for scavenging, a head
thrust fully into an animal, a beak pulling
off strips of meat, repulsed me.

Another confession: I'd always confused
conch with nautilus, something about their spirals
curling always tighter. I've read
about their histories, habitats,
reproductive habits, the uses
humans make of them. I discovered
recipes and jewelry stores, disheveled
souvenir shops and dusty museum exhibits,
but I'd never seen either
alive—the problem
I'd set out to resolve, to know
rather than know about, decline the exotic,
choose instead these spruce, sparrows, coneflowers
I pass each day.

I've Heard Stories

for Janet McAdams

My friend says everyone has a bear story, even
if it's not about a bear,
and that your story provides an index
to your personality. At first I thought
she meant your story reveals your neuroses, the origins
of those fears you wish you could
conceal, my conviction for instance that every snake
dreams itself a constrictor,
longs to squeeze the breath from my lungs,
even the green tree snake thin as twine, freshly hatched
garters squirming from their nest, even the venomous
Black Mamba which could kill me without constriction

in seconds. But when she says personality, I realize
she means personality.

I've never seen a bear outside a zoo
or taxidermist's. I've heard stories
others tell, the bear ambling across Rte. 28,
detaining the 6:30 bus, or the one ducking
behind Catskill Hall as two students
dumped their garbage, roommates from the city
who'd already fled wild
turkeys and deer. In the best
story I know, a black bear broke into an ice cream truck
three nights running. My neighbors said he liked
butterscotch topping most: it was their truck,
their driveway just a hundred yards north of mine,
but I never saw him
dip his paw into peanut butter or caramel,
bang open the freezer drawer, lurch
dizzily outside, across the cornfield toward Scotch Mountain.
I've no bear story of my own, and so you,
please, tell me yours.

22

First Breakfast in Weihai

I haven't yet learned
how to say hello, *ni hao,* or even
thank you, *xie xie ni,* so I point
to a dish of green sprouts with rice noodle threads,
a bamboo basket of dumplings,
hoping they are filled
with shrimp or pork. I choose
a square pastry stuffed with what
I expect to be spiced cabbage
but bite into sweetness,
like a donut I realize, delighted
to recognize syrupy fruit. And then,

as I glance toward the avenue, a man
hauls three hard-shell suitcases from his taxi
and one plastic bag squared with four flat boxes,
Krispy Kreme the first English words
I've seen today. He lifts the bag
delicately, so pleased that he has brought his family
such an exotic sweet.

Does a Star Know It's a Star?

the boy asked, his hand
enfolded in his father's. We're all comparing
grill brushes in the seasonal aisle
at the dollar store, one with red bristles,
one with black, when I recall
learning that in our universe, red dwarfs
are more numerous than any other star. In our universe
dwarfs and giants hang side by side,
expanding, shrinking, exploding, collapsing.
My eighth-grade earth science textbook emphasized
difference—igneous, metamorphic, sedimentary;
core, mantel, crust; cumulous, cirrus, stratus.
I memorized every list, created
my own categories, things that are bright, things
that burn, things that protect you from burning.
Duck hunting one spring, my science teacher collapsed
into the river, contributing the word corpse
to my list, things that float. This boy
picks up a lime green bucket and miniature shovel, things
you use on a beach. Things that don't
think for themselves—shovels, stars, a beating heart
or still heart. Do stars
go on vacation? he asks. Can a star get sunburned?
Every star is already on fire, his father
says, but they're so far away we can't see them
burning. Things that protect you—sunscreen, hats,
distance. I should add fathers. Things that are distant—
stars, planets, Australia, fathers. Yardsticks, mile markers, letters—
things that measure
how far away you are. Silence. Things that hold
your hand. Things that you hold in your hand—
pencils, coffee cups, emptiness. Things that disappear.

Blue Hope

Blue doesn't know
that people use
its name, lowly common noun
and ordinary adjective,
for sadness. Blue knows
morning glory, fervent bursts
of pleasure, climbing the lattice
in front of the brick house
on Hewitt St. Hearing poems or music,
The Thrill Is Gone, 'Taint Nobody's
Bizness If I Do, blue thinks aren't they wonderful,
those emotions that say *life,*
life. Blue knows its jay
bullies chickadees away from black oil
sunflower seeds, but blue loves
its jay anyway. So many of us
peck at others when we're afraid
of something we can't name.
When blue feels sad, blue
ambles down to the lake
because precision
brings blue hope—is the water
aquamarine or turquoise, indigo,
cobalt, or gentian? Is the sky
above the lake softened
by clouds or sapphire-bright?
Blue doesn't know that people
classify movies, that obscenity
rates a color. Blue knows desire and knows
that its father's eyes
captured its mother's
beating, beating heart, that its mother
loved to cradle blue-eyed babies.

Blue knows that touching your lover's skin
feels like watching a heron
lift off, reveling in its slow
elegant strength. Blue imagines
wings, muscles carrying it
skyward until it becomes indistinct,
freely watching, catching
specks of itself
flash below.

One Day in the Twenty-First Century

This morning a sparrow
flew straight
into her kitchen window,
nature's defeat once again
unintended, the thunk
so loud it startled
her arthritic dog
into barking twice.
She knows it was a sparrow
because its body
landed beside her
blue angel hosta
and she felt
its soft belly and broken neck
through her green gardening gloves.

She'd been trying
to narrow down
the hard things
to one, the photograph
of the drowned
refugee baby,
the video of a family-filled
van surrounded by orange flames,
her friend's frantic
phone call, the boy
dead, a grandson,
hung by speaker cords
from a basement pipe.

She's been living
the better part of a century
so she'd thought
the worst surely behind her.

But there's no saying
which is worst,
only which is worst now.
She's not even
succeeding at that.

The Decent Thing

Perhaps he had just sauntered
from his sister's stoop, his last joke
pitched over his shoulder,
the punch line a pun
confusing kitchen with chicken.
Perhaps he baked pastries, squeezing rosettes
onto wedding cakes, sugaring beignets
for the tourist crowd, perhaps his grandfather
had cut sugar cane in the islands
so he licked his lips the last thing, remembering
how he chewed the fiber
to its sweetness. Perhaps he taught his daughter chords
on his banjo Sunday afternoons and she showed him
how to draw a red roof atop a white house, gray smoke
curling from a black chimney.
Perhaps no one missed him.

Hit and run, likely. Maybe a stabbing,
a drive-by. Our first thought—heap of clothes,
then—corpse,
we did the decent thing
after our headlights grazed his body,
found a phone booth, declined to give
our names, drove home.

Every River Remembers the Drowned

Remember that day
when you were not
afraid, when you watched
the sun
set across the river.
Remember how you knew night
would cool, though then
warm air still settled
across your shoulders
like your lover's arm
that time
when you were not afraid.
What are you afraid of today?
Not your lover or the sun's nature
burning your skin
or the river's nature
rising and rising and tumbling
across rocks and leaving
drowned dogs and raccoons and infants
in its wake.
What are you afraid of today?
Not the world's end, an apocalypse,
but this world, the one you live in
today, those people living behind your house
who have taken your house, your son,
who have set fire
to your house, and those people living
across the river
who lock their long arms together
and say nothing and say
don't step into the river, the river
is our river.

Wreath

Everyone who ever
brushed this hair
is dead, clippings
of her mother's curls a girl wove
into a wreath, hanging it
like a watercolor or needlepoint sampler
in her family's parlor. Now
it hangs on a museum wall. Women around me
admire how each curl
turns toward the next, like blossoms
wilting in an herbalist's garden, mint leaves,
faded lavender, chamomile flowers with their bold gold centers.
Paths wind among vines, a labyrinth
to guide pilgrims. The girl

appreciated much, questioned little, trusting
God or nature or her mother
who would die of apoplexy early one morning,
her tea still steeping.

The girl's daughters begot granddaughters,
great-granddaughters who wore their hair
bobbed, all these women
visiting an exhibit, crowding me
until I can't keep
the dead safe,
steadfast, distant.

No Dinosaur Ever Saw Superior

I checked out
this book, *Geology of the Lake Superior Region,*
to learn how many millions
of years ago Superior began draining into Huron
and why all that iron and copper
compressed itself into these peninsulas,
but it says, get this,
that Superior became Superior
somewhere about 7500 years ago.
What surprises me most
is that I'm not disappointed. Of course,
a lot of other things—glaciers edging north,
marine animals dying, bedrock eroding—
happened beforehand, but it's young as bodies
of water go. It'll be around a long while yet,
I think, as if that means I'll be around
a long time, too. I know
a foolish thought

when I have one. But I'm in love
with its brutal storms, its crushed ice banks,
its 3,000,000,000,000,000 gallons of frigid water,
fifteen zeroes—million, billion, trillion, quadrillion gallons,
and I love every molecule in every one of them.

The book says Paleo-Indians
witnessed ice recede, leaving
liquid water there—here—hundreds
of feet deep, though of course it wouldn't have been
like watching a wild rosebush blossom, swollen
pink buds one day, arced petals the next,
or even like a birch tree's slow release
of seed, the seed's
germination, the sapling's thickening through years.

Still, I have to say I'm jealous—
who wouldn't want to see
aquamarine bloom across a landscape
until nothing but fresh water
shirred between your footprints and the horizon,
the largest fresh water lake in the world
emerging right where you once flung
projectiles, not exactly arrows apparently
despite our penchant for calling
every marked stone we find an arrow,
but projectiles at mastodons and moose, killing
enough of them. The book
says people found drift copper
and wore it ornamentally, as I do,
but it doesn't say how much smaller
a Paleo-Indian's foot was
than my own, or if their girls
preferred warmer inland lakes,
or if, watching the lake's surface—
rough or perilous or flat—a woman's breath
ever slowed like mine.

White Deer

Not the white of ice-blue glaciers
calving, nor the white of an old man's beard
flecked with gray and one or two black hairs,
nor the hazy white we attribute
to spirits, even those of us who deny
feeling haunted. Nothing
about these deer is translucent, these deer
who are not the white
of dandelion fluff, or canine or human
teeth, nor the white of little moons
anchoring your fingernails. Whiter than the white
of a cumulous cloud
reflecting noon sun,
if a cloud could be
solid, firm, a haunch moving
under its own volition. Their coats
not fur but pelt, heavy, tight, certain,
so bright they glow
as if lit
from within.
                          I have never seen
a white deer, just photographs
and one quiet video,
though I drive around the island,
neighborhoods where they are said to eat
rhododendrons and dogwood just like their tan
cousins, through wooded subdivisions looking,
looking. You are probably right when you say
a single vision, an ordinary animal,
its increasingly common
genetic variation, will change
nothing about my life, that a vision's
sole meaning is meaning

I've created, and you're probably right
that whatever I'm seeking already
lies within, but isn't it just possible
that a white flash leaping
over fallen oaks will illuminate
the one shadow I can't see past today?

II

McCarty's Cove

If my grandfather had never left
Kiel, I would have learned
to cook apple kugel and sauerbraten
as my father liked them. I would have enjoyed
Heinrich Böll's stories without struggling
over words like *Abschied* or *gräßlichen,* though, perhaps,
every farewell would still have felt
terrible. Walking daily down crowded streets,
I might have trained
as an interpreter, learned wood carving, or worked
on the docks, loading ships with lumber,
or hand-carved clocks, or emigrants to America.

Inhaling salt air, I would have become
one of those people who misunderstands
lakes, small or great as seas, calling them insufficient.
I would never have purchased
a laminated guide, or driven
the entire tour, Superior's breadth
stretched always to my right.

This afternoon, as winter shifts finally
toward spring, I wouldn't have imagined myself,
still barely believing my luck, kneeling
in sand between the lighthouse keeper's red house
and the cove surely meant for swimming,
filling my cupped hands
with fresh water, remembering *here,*
I live here.

Do Carnivorous Plants Experience Hunger?

This carnivorous bladderwort floats,
rootless, like a dead stem
dropped from a weakened tree, its own leaves
dark as fleas, though the water fleas
it eats, if it can be said to eat,
are often translucent, crustaceous, and always
female. An entirely female
species has, honestly, a certain appeal,
though I would not want
to see through a woman's shell
to her wormy intestine or heavy brood pouch
bursting with swollen eggs. Bladderwort
reproduce in the usual way—sepals,
petals, stamens, seeds. In the usual way, they transform
sunlight into energy but sometimes
need surplus nitrogen or carbon, as I
occasionally need more
protein or sugar. I would say to the bladderwort
if it had an eardrum, a hammer, anvil, stirrup,
cochlea, even a curve of cartilage or earlobe—I would say
that carnivorous plants are unnatural,
defying order, the taxonomic tree of life, but of course
they are natural, for we find them
impersonating a thunderstorm's detritus when we wander
to a pond, hungry for a bit of nature, if only
nature weren't so wet and muddy, if only
its terrain were better groomed,
but I don't say

any of this because I remember those
people who have called me unnatural, dismayed
at my preference for a species of females, my intrigue
with these animals—clownfish, parrotfish, water fleas in dry
    weather—
that change sex to survive, my fascination
with these plants created to digest
both light and muscle.

Wetlands

Riding to Boston, my friend watched
streams of rain curve
around dirt and bits of insect
on her window. She saw
hazy branches, leaves distorted by swollen drops.
Through the rain, she said the landscape
looked pointillist.

Today I walked three blocks
through wintery rain because I wanted to sit
in a gallery filled with landscapes.
The pond reflects bright clouds, and Mulligan Creek
shifts from aquamarine to brackish green.
A photograph reveals what could have been
sand dunes or an abandoned beach
if it weren't churned sludge
left by foresters. In this silence
and echoing footsteps, I am more alone
than I wanted to be.

Elsewhere, painters slump close,
their day spoiled by weather
or perhaps not entirely spoiled. Today they won't paint
here at the headwaters,
but one gazes west, committing the light, the shadow
to memory as if by her next visit
the land could be gone.

Chant to Lift Up the Soul of George Floyd

Smoke hovers above the old bank building,
the shoe store clearing away
its sidewalk sale, the Indian restaurant,
the Thai restaurant, the Mexican restaurant,
which yesterday served one hundred forty
orders of chicken molé. Smoke
sinks into the skinny passageway
between a new brewery and condemned diner,
beneath two floors of apartments. Smoke billows into attics,
wraps itself around photographs, scrapbooks, wedding dresses,
out through vents, out through the chink
in the wall of Harriet Jacobs' hiding place.
Smoke coats the fire escape,
every rickety step, both rusted railings,
seeps inside like haze on a tv screen
broadcasting Minneapolis set afire,
then Atlanta, L.A. We can't tell now
whether the camera films the char
of arson or the sting of tear gas. Smoke from smoldering
bricks, weight-bearing beams, red bicycle frames.
Smoke from heaps of worn tires that resist
ignition. Smoke from limbs of oak and chestnut
strong enough for a rope and the weight
it holds, smoke from the limbs
of young men. Smoke that conjures
words like *loot, riot, justifiable homicide.* Smoke from penal
    codes,
section 20-58, 20-59. Smoke from vats of bacon grease,
from shoelaces, from leather belts and cotton shirts.
Smoke from a lemon cake fresh from the oven,
swirling like condensation above ice cream, blanketing
chocolate kisses, Twizzlers, Skittles. Smoke from caps

stitched with an acronym, a president's
slogan, t-shirts stamped BLM
in 42-point sans serif font, smoke from initials
monogrammed on French cuffs, smoke
from Frederick Douglass' first
pair of long pants. Smoke curling
behind a reporter who shouts into his mic
into the tv. Smoke from King's royal reference,
Malcolm X's abandoned surname, smoke from names
common as Brown, unusual as Plessey. Smoke coats
a stray cat's orange fur, the veined ears of a shepherd mix,
every human being's skin, turning forearms,
the backs of hands gray, smoke stinging our throats,
filling our lungs, smoke we can't breathe,
we can't breathe, one night's or one week's residue
never enough to assuage
any man's pain, cheek scraping pavement,
a knee on a neck.

Mixed Media: Grief

i.

You say the eye
finds its path
toward light
in any painting,
but here
my eye follows
darkness, a blackened
disc spiraling
toward collapse. A black hole,
always an event so dense
with gravity
that nothing escapes,
not one fallen leaf,
or any living creature, not
a single wave of light,
not one particle of hope.
Could sound
penetrate gravity—a howl
of pain, of fury?

ii.

Every memory's edge
ragged like leaves
after a storm, branches
torn from their trunks.
These leaves we call
beautiful, time our travel
for peak color, try to preserve
their glory. Does a leaf die
as it falls, buoyed sometimes

by wind? Is it dead then
or somehow alive
as it settles
in the harvested garden, red
against black soil? Soon enough,
they've all crumbled, mulch
for next year's vegetation.

iii.

So we compose
elegies, an occasional
requiem, hoping
one sound,
the soprano's round syllable,
tympani's rumble, the trumpet's
fierce cry, will swell
fully enough to fill
our grief's dark cavern.

Of course I am afraid—

those creatures
we all fear—

bats—
splintery bones veining wings
as they swoop, swoop,
bulging soft underbellies
too vivid, close, tempting my mortal squeeze;

snakes—
undulant torsos, luxuriant muscle
constricting breath,
my abundant breath—

spirit
to slake constrained flesh.

Sifting Compost, I Lift a Night Crawler up into Perfect Weather with the Tine of My Pitchfork

I apologize for mornings I pierced
writhing worms with fishhooks,
quelling my empathy, blaming them
when I caught nothing. I apologize
for my first dissection, my grip
tight on my scalpel, for finding
worms uninteresting, unlike frogs
or pig fetuses with their obvious lungs,
stomachs, even their fat.

Yesterday rain ricocheted wildly
against the sidewalk, and I apologize for turning away,
disgusted by the mass of skinny and bulging worms
emerged from their saturated earth, dying
now against hot concrete. I am trying not to find
their congested squirming
repugnant, these creatures
who consume waste,
create soil.

Classroom

Randy could spell *tiger* and *wolf* and *hawk.*
Dawn's blond hair fell in ringlets; every dress shimmered.
Linda hated her freckles; Lori hated her chipped tooth; Diane
      pretended to hate the pink scar on her knee shaped like a
      rabbit.
Daniel showed the other boys a word in the dictionary.
Nobody knew that John would die when he was nineteen or that
      Liz would die when she was twenty-four.
Maureen and Jerry shared a last name, but they were not related.
      Not at all. Anyone could see just by looking.
Paul could sing the *Ave Maria* almost as well as his brother.
John could tie twelve different knots. He could make a lasso, and
      he could make a noose.
Randy learned the difference between *cell* and *sell,* between *pray*
      and *prey.*
Sheryl's mother was dead and Angela's mother wanted to move
      back to Texas and Maureen's mother wore a black slip
      under a yellow dress.
When Alan returned to school, he was bald, and then he was absent
      again.
No one knows who started the rumor that Mark's father was half
      black and half white.
Daniel said his father gave him a magazine.
Diane pretended that arithmetic was easy; Angela pretended that
      she wasn't hungry anyway; all the girls pretended not to
      hear what Daniel said.
At home, Randy could say those words about Black people and
      Mexicans without getting in trouble.
Linda said *yes* and *yes* and *yes* because what good was *no*; Dawn
      said *no* in secret; Sheryl kept quiet.
Randy learned to spell *rifle* and *bullet.*

Mockingbird

In another life, you'll master
keyboards, the harpsichord, play fugues,
fantasias, the *Goldberg Variations*
so flawlessly and often you'll dream
you're Bach's mother, dying again,
orphaning him again. When you wake,
a boy will hover at your bedside, your own
son, your youngest, hushed
as snow, stiff
as an icicle afraid to drip.
You'll want to shake him, hiss
buck up, but you won't. What you'll do
is sing, some old song, *Mama's
gonna buy you,* until he sings too,
both of you raspy-voiced, tone-deaf,
softly, softly singing.

Cord

My brother saved for success. He saved his savings and his savings grew. He saved string from a broken necklace, rubber bands from newspapers, straw from the barn floor. He saved his family from disaster. Holding the thrumming umbrella above his own head, he saved his daughter from lightning strikes. He saved tomatoes from bottom rot and corn from weevils. He saved hollow bones for a dog and unwashed tuna cans for cats. For the birds he saved berries and bacon grease, and he saved the smells in his shut up kitchen. He saved his son from anger, and his own twinges of rage he saved in a metal bucket for another son to tip over as he dangled by a short cord from his closet door.

Boundary Water

Dark sky,
dark waves. Rain
spatters the lake, becomes
the lake. No thunder—I
can linger. Some forms
dissolve, but my body
drifts, half submerged,
half breaking
the surface.

One dragonfly hovers

above Presque Isle's iron-gray
outcroppings, its near wing
a smudge of indigo at the edge of my eye,
blurring like the shade
of the dead friend I thought
I saw crossing the sidewalk.

Days like this, the almost real
is more real than anything real.
My breath caught, seeing her
grasp the wrought-iron railing. Then, I watched
a stranger latch a gate. Today,

the wave's pace quickens while water
deepens from ultramarine to midnight.
Small creatures shift imperceptible antennae
as wings whirr, then disappear.

Words for the Past

She was the daughter, wasn't she,
not the granddaughter, definitely not
a niece? She couldn't button
her tan coat across her girth
even as snow blew
thickly across the sidewalk, blocking their car.
Did she talk much? I don't remember her
saying anything. The daughter,
definitely, but how was she
part of us, not a single name in common?
Her grandmother was my great-grandmother's
sister. Her grandmother was your mother-in-law's
great aunt. Did they drink?
The only oddness I remember, the dark
mess inside their house. When we saw them last,
I was six or seven. Now I think
someone, maybe the father, Ray wasn't it,
must have been a drinker. I only ever remember
one of them, the aunt who never married,
ever saying anything, scolding me
for refusing my nap. This was before. I remember it
because my mother was sleeping in a Saginaw hospital,
soon to bring my sister, the last of us, home. Indignation
is the only word for my response, being told
to nap, though of course I didn't possess
the word yet. I dreaded going
over there, the house so dark,
sinister, another word I couldn't use
until later to describe what I felt.
I know the words now if not the facts,
nor when they died, nor how, for surely they're all dead,
as surely as I'm sitting here asking questions
of a man who would have answered
if I'd thought to ask in time.

Inside

My friend says heroin smothers
bad thoughts,
so I say bad thoughts
like why does it rain
so many Saturdays or like
I wish my shabby neighbor
and every one of his yapping dogs
would drown in a raging
muddy torrent together and be buried
together in one heaping putrid grave.
My friend says the first one

and so I think
about rain clouds gathering
close like the quilt your grandmother
stitched the first year of her long marriage
folded at the foot of your bed, its border
faded, fraying, but the silhouettes
of rabbits and cats still visible in its square-inch squares,
rain clouds fading gray to white or shading
into black, rain that keeps you
inside warm, nostalgic, reading
a long novel, *The Brothers
Karamazov* or *The Old Curiosity Shop,* thinking
how rain heralds
new seasons, spring
into summer, fall into winter, not every change pleasant
but pleasant enough for you're still
here aren't you buttoning your flannel shirt,
black watch plaid, narrow cuffs, banded collar—
why does a shirt make you feel so good?—

you're here watching rain
meander down your window, curving
as streams curve toward an easier way, its tap,
tap reminiscent of some song
you learned years earlier to help you
remember colors, how vibrant the purple, blue, yellow
became once you learned their names, indigo,
how you liked saying it, *indigo.*
Your mouth vibrated with vowels,
shimmering like the green and scarlet
leaves do now through this watery
weather that could be so
discouraging, so irritating, but isn't, isn't. It keeps you
here inside where you've always wanted to stay.

Water Music, 7-17-1717

Its first performance: a barge
laden with musicians, the concertmaster squeezed too close
to the conductor, the Thames
rolling softly, narrowing at its curves, only slightly
fragrant with waste, the king
reclined on another barge, anxious to hear, drinking
with duchesses, a countess, an earl. The prelude
twirls against his ear for the first time, that ear
scarred from his early taste
for pugilism and weary
of jokes others repeat, his son's impatience
for his death. The king asks
his musicians to play and play again
until their lips strain with thin cuts and their fingertips
crack open. The composer listens
past the water's hush
against its shore, listens, revises, watches
men and women born to rule, recline, jockey for power,
fearing patricide, regicide more than death itself.
The king lets out a guttural laugh, seems
to swallow a belch, and the composer
glances down, spies a cluster of leaves, mostly still
green, clinging to his shoe. How slowly
the earth turns, season to season, yet how quickly
time passes. He will drink tonight
and be merry, cheered by such robust strings, his own music
more boisterous than any knowledge of mortality.

Ferris Wheel at the Abandoned Boardwalk

The last boy who sat in car 17
was not afraid until
he looked out to sea, saw
foaming waves roll beachward then ripple back
as if they, too, distrusted edges. The boy remembered
how the struts creaked at first,
lifting him up, and then quieted
until he felt himself floating. Leaning back,
his car rocking softly, he wondered
if, from the ground, he resembled the sky, almost purple
at dusk. His pockets harbored sand,
one green stone, three scallop shells
waves had left for him
or someone else to find after high tide.
He would clean them later and leave them
to bleach on his windowsill
where last summer he had left a polaroid
of himself waving from this same Ferris wheel.
Rain had wrinkled its finish, and the sun
had faded his image into a green and purple blur.

.

Balloon

I stoop to tie my shoes, the neon
yellow laces frayed at their ends, leaking fine threads
like hair that won't stay combed, and I reach
to catch the yellow threads floating up and through
my closed screen door, then drifting, light
enough to be buoyed without the least breeze.
I grasp one thread, grab on like I'm holding
a balloon, a yellow smiley-faced, don't worry, be happy
balloon, and feel my bare feet
lift out of my shoes and off the grass and feel
the arches of my feet cool and then curl
around themselves, my feet small
lower-case o's, my legs exclamation points above them.
Children point up toward me,
a boy hoisting his striped shirt above his belly, a girl
clutching a trio of dandelions, their parents
lifting their hands like salutes
to block the glare, squinting, confused, as if they can't see
me. I've floated past
the lighthouse, the breakwall, the Coast Guard tugboat.
I'm waving now with my left hand, waving
at three otters splashing each other near the boat launch,
at kayaks and kayakers and their yellow life vests,
the shipwreck upside down on the lake floor since 1869,
waving, waving until all I see
is the sun's wide ray, tempting
as a playground slide and angled
straight toward the beach
in case I want, someday, to return.

Bear

At first I saw slumped shadow,
a dark just darker than autumn darkness.
Then I distinguished sloped shoulder, snout,
bulky hind leg. I saw her head tilt.
I saw the garbage cans
where she'd dragged them. She sat
a while longer, eating, not eating, as I watched
from our lightless kitchen. Time shifted
as when a river
begins to flood. I watched her
amble toward a brake of oak saplings.
I saw her merge into night until the space
that had held her held
only night, a globe of darkness
I wished to enter
but could only dispel.

Inland Sea

No one has drowned in Superior
since October. Crisp water nudges its long shore,
an inland sea we say in my cold country's cold interior.

Since October, every death wearies me wearier,
jagged, cutting, years from safely smooth sea glass washed ashore.
No one has drowned in Superior

who didn't fight to live. Who'd have thought me the worrier,
yet I sense this one's daring, that one's bravado, my fear a feeble
    oar
against an inland sea. We say in my cold country's cold interior

fate is as good as grace, and no one's luck is linear.
We talk of storms, shipwrecks, copper, legends, iron ore.
No one has drowned in Superior

without knowing force, power, surrender. Their soul's soft-spoken
    courier
floats upward, singing, invisible, her open arms offering one spirit
    more
to an inland sea, we say in my cold country's cold interior.

Nature's account marks each element equal, nothing inferior,
nothing exceptional, save our false folklore:
no one has drowned in Superior,
an inland sea, my cold country's cold interior.

Northern Michigan, Late Afternoon, Early September

i.
Among reeds, a juvenile crane
stills himself,
listening to thin splashes.
One faint canoeist
follows the shore.

ii.
Each crane takes slow care
extending its leg, stretching
through obscure water.

iii.
A loon invisibly calls.
Cranes lift themselves,
their shadows
crossing the canoe.

iv.
Silence.
A rustling breeze.
Silence.

III

After Reading John S. Willett's *Book of American Trivia*

Not every day but most days, my wife
asks me to open a jar, her arthritic hand
fleeting across mine. Pasta sauce, raspberry jam,
chunky salsa, farmhouse chutney. I ask her
if she knows people once used wax
to seal glass bottles. Behind our conversation, I hear
fruit jars clanking against plates and cutlery.
I hear wheels rutting the road from my ancestors' wagons
as they jostle through New England, Pennsylvania,
across Ohio, Indiana. I hear crows
object to homesteaders, chipmunks scutter through leaves,
a nearly silent lizard scratch one leg before it catches
hold of a shaded axle. One of the women
shouts *stop, just stop* in northeastern Nebraska.
So they stop, generations
of them plowing fields, husking corn. I hear
my father ask my mother how many
tomatoes she will can this year, how many beans
she will freeze. Steam blurs the kitchen. Tomato peelings
drop into the sink. Plump flesh, grained like muscle,
slides into quart jars, one pink globe slumped against another,
    heaped
to the threaded glass mouths, John Landis Mason's
favorite invention. He died broke
like most people who change our lives
for the better. Someone should have told him: renew
your patent and keep
your lizard farm secret, all those captive reptiles
making him criminal. His daughters said *stop*,
but he wouldn't hear. He appreciated their colorful skin, the small
gecko's toes, rounded as buds. Their names
pleased him—chameleon, iguana, skink—and please me too. They
    ate

so little, crickets or dandelion greens, and drank even less.
When the sheriff ambled into his yard
and unfolded the warrant, Mason was watching a wood lizard
tongue mist from the underside of chicory.
He wouldn't have predicted
children would twist caps
on his jars after they'd captured
lightning bugs, pollywogs, garter snakes, so many creatures
inadvertently killed. But last night
when I opened a bottle of ginger ale, its fizz
misted my hands, sweetening the entire kitchen.
I wondered which of my relatives
first felt carbonation in their mouths
or took ice cubes for granted.
I'd never thought enough about sealed jars,
their threaded mouths, to praise the threads' creator
who made it possible for me
to perform this small delightful favor.

Foreground

I'm told it's possible to train your eye to see
near and far simultaneously. Consciously focused,
I watch your reflection
overlap mine in this window, you gazing
toward mourning doves,
plump ground feeders. I see your reflection

and I see the doves, the grass, gleeful squirrels,
cat preparing to pounce. I can look
at the arch of your eyebrow,
at the cat as she leaps, misses,
back to your forehead, your fingers smoothing
a twist of hair, but some detail remains
invisible. I can see fresh growth
sprouting from our blue spruce
only if I look past, not at, the light leaves
of our aging oak, the white window frame

carrying our reflections, two women
gazing past themselves as something
flickers across the dusky lawn.

Three Views of Flight

i.

Gulls plunge toward my raised hands, the undersides
of their wing feathers lined with darkness. One remains
tilted against a neighbor's gabled roof,
one more attached to the near maple's cragged branch, or is it
a leaf, dead and clinging?

ii.

You say the abandoned wasp's nest
reveals nature's drive toward order.
I forgive the swarm, their stinging welts,
but I cannot ease
my panic, their excess
crawling among identical trembling bodies.
I prefer the empty hive
to the pulsing mass, and more,
I prefer the image, a painting shaded
boldly enough to convey its art's artifice.

iii.

Through jagged slats, the sky
soars. Nothing
floats or falls, dives toward me or away.
My vision fills, a bare
hayloft, dust motes, the barn's collapsing
roof, the blue, the blue.

Seven Meditations on Romance

From the hotel balcony, I watch
one fin break through surf—dolphin
or shark?

Early on, a transplanted shrub
sleeps, its dreams
entangled with images of roots
curving around stones, shards of pottery, rusted nails,
other roots.

Hunched in its cocoon, a caterpillar
splits its body open, curls itself
inside out. Creepy, but natural.

My lover asks me
to write a poem about her. This poem
is not that poem.

The heart
is just as dark
as other organ meats,
though perhaps it sometimes
tastes less bitter.

Yes, a few animals mate
for life. And in some species, fathers
nurture their young. Many of us
have seen a satisfied female
snap her lover's neck
after sex. We slow
the tape to watch again.

Would it have turned out differently
if Jocasta had married the Moor
or Desdemona solved the riddle
of the sphinx?

Illustrated Cookbook

Asparagus framed with parsley, frothy
leaves circling thick spears. We imagine
crisp green illustrations replacing these
charcoal drawings. Eggplant, pears, their curves
fuller than any fruit in any garden.
We imagine our fingers searching for bush beans,
pole beans, recall sugar snap peas, their plump pods
plumper every day, bold bell peppers beside them,
green flaming into red. Peaches and plums,
seamed along one side, cupped
in our palms, their ripe juice
dripping past our wrists, our fingers and forearms
sticky with nectar. We imagine our tongues
sucking pulp. Oh cherry tomatoes, oh
better boys and early girls, every one of you so
globular, tugging your stems
earthward, as if all you desire
is to sink into warm soil, be held up
by warm soil, your flesh ready
to burst through its skin.

Literacy

Alphabets lead easily to reading, you once
believed, with their clear categories, long or short vowels,
consonants, diphthongs plunging from your mouth the way a long
  slide
drops you into the community pool. Language provides such
  generous
exceptions to every rule, as frustrating as your buxom aunt
from Tallahassee who arrives always on the wrong day, laden with
  gifts,
greeting you with your sister's name, her pockets trailing kleenex,
  her bemused
husband forgotten at the last rest stop. Consider the silent e,
  consider the homonym:
is d-o-v-e the peaceable bird or the past tense of your swan dive,
jocular belly flop, comical pike, into the community pool? And
  why is m-o-v-e
kindly called a sight rhyme of trove and love? You mumble and
  move awkwardly,
lips numbed by chlorine and cold, anglicizing joie de vivre,
mispronouncing mauve which does rhyme with dove, though who
  would guess,
not the lifeguard or clown hawking creamsicles or the girl singing
  her color song: red and
orange, green and blue, shining yellow, purple too. She stares at
  your puffing
pink-cheeked aunt, covets her billowy tunic, its massive flowers
  not red, not
quite purple, each center knotted gold, every leaf a wisp of
  emerald. The girl delights in puns,
recites knock-knock jokes until you refuse to say who's there and
  then
she asks it herself, who *is* there? Nobody, you say,
tempted to tell the story of Odysseus, the Cyclops, the Greeks'
  escape

under the bellies of sheep. She prefers fairies, Dr. Seuss, the Pied
    Piper's
village of charmed rats, though she snuggles up to your aunt
who brings improbable books to the pool, *The Autobiography of
    Malcolm
X, Custer Died for Your Sins,* Mao's *Little Red Book,* the thick
    green
Yiddish dictionary she swiped from her grandmother's nursing
    home,
Zelda Anne signed inside the front cover, with a date, and a word
    she can't read.

The Tape Measure Instructs the Carpenter

You measure a window frame
down to a thirty-second of an inch,
a doorframe only to a quarter.
Some things just need to fit
tighter than others—if there's a reason,
it's not worth thinking about. You need to measure
from the inside of the frame for blinds but from the outside
for curtains. Most things that can be measured
you can figure out
easily enough. It's the things that can't be,
that won't arrange themselves in proper rows,
that guarantee you trouble. A doorknob
for instance is simple enough to install—
they're all standardized—but who can tell you
which one will attract the thief?
A garage needs to be roomier now, though cars
have grown cramped, especially when a desperate man
leans his seat back, closes his eyes, leaves
the engine running. V-8, V-6, diesel or regular
hardly matters. He likely doesn't have a wife
anymore or an oldest son to find him.
He totaled everything up, how much
gas in the tank, how many cubic feet
in the garage. Then he said a prayer
for Mrs. Fromee who taught him his times tables,
and Miss Galbraith who taught him geometry,
and Mr. Owens who taught him physics,
and then he began to count
backwards from one hundred, drifting off
as he did every night
somewhere in the seventies.

Archipelago

In Alaska, it's illegal to kill a crow
sometimes, in some zones. We grieve death until we die.
People say crows carry souls past despair, through woe.

We grieve grandparents, suicidal classmates, murdered boys, a
    miscarried embryo,
drowned refugees, diseased bats, extinct species we can't quantify.
In Alaska, it's illegal to kill a crow

except for food. If hunger drives you to trap a fox, shoot a doe,
still some animals survive on beauty, glasswing moths, an emerald
    dragonfly.
People say crows carry souls past despair, through woe.

People say blue jays are bullies and doves are holy. Isn't wind
    holy, and snow
and blizzards that obscure each bird, every bear, even the glorious
    sky
in Alaska? It's illegal to kill a crow

or so I've been told. Maybe that was true once long ago.
My spirits were lifted by a feathery creature with a swift wing and
    sharp eye.
People say crows carry souls past despair, through woe.

In this world, evil swirls as a dark sea, heaven but its archipelago.
We choose beliefs to defy or ideas to deify.
In Alaska, it's illegal to kill a crow.
People say they carry souls past despair, through woe.

The Dreamer's Wish Is Never Fulfilled in the Dream

When you find yourself wandering a strange city, cautious,
unsettled, search for cobblestoned streets.
They will not lead you home, but they will lead you
past the brownstone with its wrought-iron gate, its garden
of purple coneflowers and globe thistles and everlasting. You can
    eat
your sandwich on a bench across the boulevard, the one you chose
from the narrow shop under its green awning—
prawns with avocado, chicken tikka, egg salad with rocket on
    wheat.
The day will be sunny or overcast, or a light rain
will spatter the pavement. When you drop the knocker on the
    arched door,

don't be startled that the woman who responds
recognizes you. You each believe yourselves misplaced
in time, but time is measured
differently here. The house will be nothing
like your own, its woodwork dark, its silence
weighted with comfort, and the china cup
she carries to serve your coffee ornately
traced with gold. You are still

lost, but now you are her guest,
this quiet woman who places a tray of pastries
between you, unfolding her napkin as she eases herself
onto her brocade sofa, waiting
as you begin to speak.

The Poet Responds to Her Lover, the Painter Who Claims Words Languish Beside Color, Texture, Shadow and Light

Blue, for instance.

Think: Lake Superior, Lake Michigan, Grand Traverse Bay,
      damp sand cooling your soles, water
      soothing your skin, your spirit.
      Ripples, reflected sunlight stings your eyes,
      even the memory of it.

Think: ellipse of sky among clouds,
      how as you descended Coe Hill you caught
      your glimpse, three cloud patterns, three weather formations
      shading Otsego's valleys.

Listen as I list: cobalt, cornflower, delft, indigo,
          turquoise, topaz, sapphire,
          lapis lazuli.
Listen as *blue* dissolves into *blew* or *bleu*.

Once I overheard my grandmother confess
she sometimes thought she saw
figures treading the sky, robed men and women
conversing fearlessly.

My daughter, more fearless than I, loves
bats, snakes, every species of rodent; more observant,
she fingers a stone, whispers *lapis lazuli*.

Think: snow drifting through dim light, spruce fading into evening
  as evening
      sinks into night.

I say *jay* and you will recall its squawk, chickadees
      fleeing the feeder. You will recall your story,
      twelve hawks clawing feathers
      from one bloodied jay.
I say *heron* and you will remember our creek where it curves into
   the river,
      the bird's calm attention, listening, still,
      how gracefully it unfolded
      its wings,
      disappeared.

Golden Gate

He'd expected to feel
buoyed by some secret force
until the bay received him gently,
gloriously. Dawn's early light
ricocheted from red beams, steel cables;
a beautiful suicide he imagined
in the coroner's script, the eulogist's voice.

Never recovered, his body
became feast for scavenging crustaceans that couldn't care
whether his irises glittered hazel or simple brown.
Crabs sucked at his eyeballs, his fatty cheeks,
scuttled across his sternum toward bloated fingertips.

The corpse discovered that day instead
had not hit feet first; her ribs
plunged into spleen, heart, lungs,
saving her
the panic of the drowned. Her gauzy blouse
shredded at the shoulder seam, stray threads
tangling into gray hair. Some years later,

two children would discover her bifocals
twisted in a heap of driftwood. She left
no note and no one
reported her missing. While the children,
first the boy, then the girl modeled her glasses,
solemn as owls, a young bank teller
drove across the dull Bay Bridge, steered north
toward the world's most glamorous suspension.

He'd taped a note to his dash, typed,
unsigned, as if to taunt
his mother who would recall
yesterday's insult—she cared
more for her conspiracy theories
than for her children. She would consider

leaping herself, would imagine
each of the two hundred twenty feet
between the short railing and the sweet tide,

would even stroll the walkway, greeting the patrolman
who waved like a stranger. Every day
for twelve weeks she strode one direction,
then its opposite, resigning herself
finally to this life, its brilliance, its regret.

That Delicious Word

Were you imagining honey, Walt Whitman, a land flowing with it, so intense half a teaspoon suffices to sweeten your breakfast tea? Our honeybee colonies are afflicted Walt Whitman; we envision blossoms dropping from stalks, pollen scattered uselessly on dry soil. But we believe in famine the way we believe in leprosy.

Did you intend a subtler flavor? Clotted cream spread lightly across scones, currants, nuggets of apricot, candied ginger, small enough promises. We've never imagined you subtle.

Last night, Walt Whitman, I ate goat's eye beans flavored with cumin. They were delicious, and the posole was delicious, a full peppery bowl that set my tongue deliciously afire. Is this what you meant Walt Whitman, that we shall want to eat death slowly again and again?

My grandfather was called Walter too. I hope he found death delicious but I do not think he did.

Some people crave salt and some crave bitterness—broccoli rabe, mustard greens—but my palate has not so matured.

My lover's mouth is filled with sores Walt Whitman, from a disease that might have killed her. She finds applesauce delicious, and coconut yogurt. I bring her palm-sized bowls, each spoonful promising life, life. I simmer chicken soup, butter a boiled egg, every bite promising.

For thirty years I have fancied rattlesnake, though I try not to believe death is so ghastly I would gloat after putting it in my mouth.

Eye to Eye

Give me that sidelong look, give me
that crinkled eye, curved as an almond, dark
as vanilla. Oh surrender your glance, your gaze,
your chestnut eye, sweet as kiwi, round as coconut.
Eye like agate, like geode a girl
breaks open, clapping for what hides
inside. Eye of newt dropped into a bubbling potion,
inflicting mischief or love or love's revenge.
Eye of giant squid whose courting habits
are discourteous, eye of Brookesia micra who inhabits
an uninhabited island, her mating rituals
never seen by a naked
human eye. I call you
apple of my eye and so can call you
Honeycrisp, Ambrosia, my Delicious.
Give me your majestic eye, your exceptional eye, your superlunary
    eye.
Give me your sumptuous eye, your transcendent eye. Emerson
    advised
he would become a transparent eyeball, but I prefer
your opaque amber iris, your perfect pupil.
So long as we can breathe, or eyes can see,
drink to me only. Raise a toast
with demitasse cups, crystal tumblers, cut-glass goblets.
Lift your magnums, your Jeroboams, your Nebuchadnezzars.
Be my witness. Eye that watches me tumble
clumsily as Jack or Jill, fall greatly off a wall,
eye that puts me back together again.

Peregrination

In my house—I respond
to the student who asks why
can't I just say walk?—
we say we're going to perambulate
the dog because the dog
understands the word walk and barks himself
into a frenzy if ever he hears
walk; he even knows
w-a-l-k, so we've brainstormed
synonyms, for example mosey which clarifies his style
now that he's seven and August heat
discourages the hip-hop skitter
and pounce he practiced his first fall,
attacking each red leaf
flitting across the sidewalk as if it were
some invasive rodent. And walk insufficiently
suggests his gait—he swings
and swaggers; freshly bathed,
he sashays across our one-lane bridge,
amusing drivers patient enough to watch
his dainty strut as he sniffs
clumps of fur stuck in tar,
crushed soda cans, milkweed
thrusting itself through gravel. He lunges
up the dark meandering root-snarled path
because after blizzards he's permitted
to leap drift to drift, cooling his pink belly
as I straggle and stumble, sweating through wool and down,
pausing to identify tracks: deer, skunk, turkey, dog.
Warm evenings, he backs his haunches
into stinkweed, prowls soggy ditches, shambles
through alfalfa and fresh-cut hay.

Squirrels scuttle from ash to oak, safely
beyond his curiosity or the interest
of my student who's trudging now
in his mind up the impossibly
steep steps of this assignment,
schlepping instructions from table to carrel to desk,
limping, staggering under their yoke
while I saunter home, oblivious, indifferent,
because it's easy for me, he's certain,
this jaunt, this stroll, this ramble.

Burned

The Great Marquette Fire, 1868

Three wooden shipping docks.

Wooden shops along Front Street and Main Street and Superior Street. Every wooden building between Fourth Street and the lake.

David Scoville's hardware store, every hammer and handsaw, bags of licorice he kept for children, all his penny nails.

One girl's hope chest lit up like a fiery crown, its elaborate trick lock smoldered to ash, her doilies, embroidered pillow cases, three shades of green thread marking leaves and stems, one appliqued quilt. Her darning needles.

Mr. McGilligan's corpse inside its casket.

First National Bank though not its cash, for Peter White filled canvas bags with bills, coins, a sheaf of records, threw it all onto a skiff and ordered his assistant to row past the shipping lane, to return only after every glowing ember collapsed into ash.

Horse manure left in the streets or shoveled under wooden sidewalks.

Five hundred tons of pig iron if pig iron can be said to burn. Pig iron but no pigs or cattle or horses, for every living thing survived.

Mr. McGilligan's casket steadied on a dock, waiting to be loaded onto the next boat to Ontario.

Milton's poems, Calvin's sermons, that bestseller *Uncle Tom's Cabin,* all fifteen hundred books inside the city library, and the library.

Philo Everett's furniture hauled out to Third Street for safety. Sparks showered his oak hutch anyway, his four cane chairs, his horsehair sofa.

One altar, wainscoting, a few dozen pews. First Presbyterian Church delayed its first service until Christmas. Peter White, David Scoville, and Philo Everett worshipped elsewhere.

The newspaper office, every report of scandal, marriage, church suppers, eminent visitors.

The small New Testament inside Mr. McGilligan's pocket.

What didn't burn: a butcher shop, a southside hardware store, every residence south of Superior Street and all of the residents. Each person lived to describe the longest dock, hundreds of feet out into the water, bejeweled with flame, how astonishing it was, how terrifying, how beautiful.

Blood

My father used words
like *alfalfa* and *acre*
as easily as I said *street* or *stoplight*
or *fire hydrant.* Sometimes he harnessed *suspicion*
into a verb. I *suspicion*
he'd say, *that's not all there is to that story*
about every story distinguishing guilt
from innocence. Cousins on his side corrected me
for calling their road
a street, chastened me
for my sharp vowels—*address,*
excited, milk, house.

We stumbled
across a pasture, following one cow
as she wandered toward the barn,
her back legs patchy
with blood. She must have birthed
her calf early and left it
where it lay. Not understanding
what blood meant, I felt
my skin prickle
with an irritated embarrassed

betrayal. Decades later, I catch myself
again, anxious
that I don't know such simple things
as the difference between a combine and a cultivator,
whether my cousins milked Jerseys or Guernseys,
who I'm including when I say
extended family, what words
I should have said to my father
those years he lived.

Year of Water

i

My palms glow
with chrysanthemums
circling lit wicks
as I bend
to the Ganges,
release my bouquet.

ii.

Back home, pagodas
of snow
crest the bird feeders.
Cardinals flash near
one window, then out of the frame.

iii.

Ice splinters against mud,
crystals dissolving
into slush—was that
this year or last?

iv.

We begin
thinking of tomato plants
and pole beans, check the hose
for leaks.

v.

Spring rises. Sitting
outside, I recall
the priest's blessing at Pushkar Lake, above
one ghat, red and gold thread
knotted around my wrist.

vi.

Her water breaks.

vii.

Sparrows swoop
to the stone birdbath. Their wings
scoop refracted
sunlight from the moist hollow.

viii.

Thunderclouds crowd the sky;
dry creeks gush, then flood.

ix.

My desires sundered
by dead grass etched with frost,
I receive the awe of autumn's
patterns, resist the knowledge
of what will come.

x.

A waterspout dips into the world's
largest lake. Viewed from this distance, chaos
looks mystical.

xi.

Soon, soon,
my body will return
to earth, my longing
for immersion fulfilled.

xii.

What good news
do snow angels
deliver? Every flake blesses
your bare head.

The Road to Happiness

a streak of light visible upon a breeze-wrinkled surface of water is called
"The Road to Happiness"

—Monte Reel

Cresting the hill west of Seymour,
past shiny signs proposing chicken sandwiches,
breakfast all day, larger coffee, biscuits,
new flavors, and past two Chinese
buffets rumored to be closing
forever, and past the auto parts store,
insurance agency, and cheap hair salon
where young women wax
my eyebrows, and always past a snowplow
spitting sand and the car wash that opens
only after temperatures rise
above twenty, and past the school bus
carrying cheerleaders to the township
and the pick-up stacked with storm windows,

I look up to see, again, the lake
stretching, I know, to another country,
and I take its blue measure,
and I take in its wind-brushed
surface, its narrow breakwater crusted
with ice, clouds dropping to a near horizon, and I know
I don't want to live forever,
but I want to live
here forever.

About the Author

Lynn Domina is the author of several books, including two previous collections of poetry, *Corporal Works* and *Framed in Silence*. She serves as Creative Writing Editor of *The Other Journal* and teaches English at Northern Michigan University. After stints in lower Michigan, Alabama, Illinois, and New York, she lives now with her family in Marquette, Michigan, along the beautiful shores of Lake Superior, where she hopes to stay for the rest of her life.

Read More
www.lynndomina.com